THE LAYMAN'S GUIDE TO

ELECTRONIC

EAVESDROPPING

THE LAYMAN'S GUIDE TO

ELECTRONIC

EAVESDROPPING

HOW IT'S DONE AND SIMPLE WAYS TO PREVENT IT

TOM LARSEN

PALADIN PRESS
BOULDER, COLORADO

Also by Tom Larsen:

Bench-Tested Circuits for Surveillance and Countersurveillance Technicians

More Bench-Tested Circuits: Innovative Designs for Surveillance and Countersurveillance Technicians

The Layman's Guide to Electronic Eavesdropping:
How It's Done and Simple Ways to Prevent It
by Tom Larsen

Copyright © 1996 by Tom Larsen

ISBN 0-87364-879-X
Printed in the United States of America

Published by Paladin Press, a division of
Paladin Enterprises, Inc.
Gunbarrel Tech Center
7077 Winchester Circle
Boulder, Colorado 80301 USA
+1.303.443.7250

Direct inquiries and/or orders to the above address.

Visit our Web site at www.paladin-press.com

Contents

Warning

This book is *for informational purposes only*. Neither the author nor the publisher condones or is responsible for the illegal use of information contained in this book.

Dedication

To my wife, for her wisdom and patience. Also, to Pat, Ward, and T.M. for helping me break into this industry.

Preface

The purpose of this book is to inform average people about how an individual, or a group of individuals, can successfully spy on them without their knowledge. I will cover some of the basic methods and do it in such a way that a nontechnical person can understand. It is my sincere hope that most people who read this book will be able to prevent themselves from being victimized by electronic surveillance experts.

What is my primary motivation? Too often I meet security personnel, private investigators, and clients who are laboring under a mountain of Hollywood-inspired myths. It is well known to industry insiders that most people who do electronic countermeasures sweeps do not understand the basic parameters of their sweep equipment or phone line basics. Most of them do not even know a transistor from a resistor.

This is not a book on how to wiretap or bug. It is designed to show people how their privacy can be invaded, using the philosophy that "to be forewarned is to be forearmed." I will not dedicate much space to countermeasures. Most countermeasures are just a matter of common sense, and any technical countermeasures should be left to a professional who knows the difference between a transistor and a resistor and how they are used in an electronic circuit.

Sit back, relax, and have a spot of tea as you read this informative book and watch those Hollywood myths fall by the wayside.

P.S. When analyzing any suspected bugging or tapping situation, ask yourself the following question: What are the motive, means, and opportunity of the suspected eavesdropper(s)?

Telephones

It is estimated that 90 percent of all important details about your life goes out over phone lines. Telephones have "done in" more folks than you can shake a stick at. They can be tapped in dozens of ways at very little cost (in most cases). One hour of recorded phone conversations is equal to ten or more hours of conversation. If a subject is very sensitive and incriminating, do not talk about it over the telephone.

The following is a sample of the ways in which someone might intercept your phone conversations. Let's begin at your home or office and work our way down the phone line and eventually to the phone company's central switching office, or CO for short. I will examine some simple phone line parameters (basics) before we begin.

HOME TELEPHONES

Your home phone plugs into a wall jack. From there the wires terminate at a connector block known as a surge protector, or demark point. The surge protector is usually housed in a plastic (modern) or metal (old style) housing, which is easily opened. The surge protector is usually mounted on the outside wall of the house.

Phone conversations are generally carried out over two wires known as a "talk path." These two

Subscriber interface or surge protector box located on the outside wall of a private residence. This is one of the later versions (late 1980s).

wires start at your telephone and ultimately terminate at the phone company's CO. There may be a half a dozen or more easily accessible connector blocks, which are housed in a variety of metal cabinets on telephone poles or on concrete pads on street corners. These connector blocks are ideal places to place taps off the premises. Many of these connector blocks are housed in cabinets so large that one could hide several tape

The box on the left is a splice box, or pedestal, for two private residences in an area where there are underground utilities. It contains a connector block where phone lines appear. You'd better pray that this is in your yard and not the yard of a neighbor whom you are feuding with.

This is a splice box in a rural area. It will probably service about a half-dozen subscribers.

recorders in them (one for each line) with room to spare. When you're out driving around, keep your eyes open for them and you will understand what I'm talking about.

The phone company's CO could be anywhere from 100 feet to 10 miles downwire from your premises. In every major city there are at least two dozen or more COs serving the community. When you talk on the phone with your next-door neighbor, your voice transmission hits the CO, then it goes out of the central switching office on your neighbor's wire pair all the way back to his house and vice versa. Even though your wire pair may be housed in the same cable

CHAPTER 1
Telephones

An area interface box is usually mounted on a concrete pad and is filled with connector blocks containing phone lines. According to phone tech manuals, this should take care of a 1/2-mile by 1/2-mile residential area.

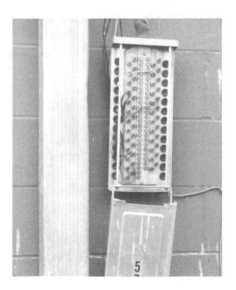

Talk about being vulnerable! This splice box was found behind a small strip mall.

sheath as your neighbor's, all of your conversations go through the central switching office that services your area.

When you talk with someone who is not serviced by your CO, your conversations may hit several central switching offices. When you talk long distance, there is an 80 percent chance that your conversation will be carried on easily intercepted microwave links or satellite links. There are Fortune 500 companies that market microwave/satellite phone conversation/data transmission interception equipment.

When a tap is placed at the central switching office, there is no way to detect its existence— period! Most properly designed and constructed telephone taps cannot be heard or detected with electronic instrumentation when they are placed at the central switching office. There is absolutely no way of detecting whether someone is monitoring the microwave link or the satellite link of a phone conversation/data transmission. You'd better believe that there is, indeed, random monitoring of microwave/satellite phone and data transmissions from time to time by government, industry, and private individuals.

Here is a simple method of tapping that may be employed by a spouse, roommate, or significant other who has access to the premises. They can place an automatic tape starter (which usually costs about $24.95 and is sold at many electronics stores) and a tape recorder behind or underneath a large, hard-to-move piece of furniture that has a telephone jack behind it. They could also place it in the attic or the basement, wherever the phone lines run. All they have to do is cut off the modular end of the automatic tape starter, attach alligator clips, and hook them anywhere across the phone line. For those of you who do not know what an automatic tape starter is, it turns on the tape recorder when the phone is picked up and then shuts the recorder off when the phone is hung up. Its purpose is to tape a conservation without having any "dead tape" time.

A device that very effectively thwarts this kind of phone tapping is a voltage spreader. It keeps the voltage at or above 20 volts DC (direct current), thus keeping the automatic tape starter from turning on. However, these voltage spreaders will not work against voice-activated or radio frequency-type taps.

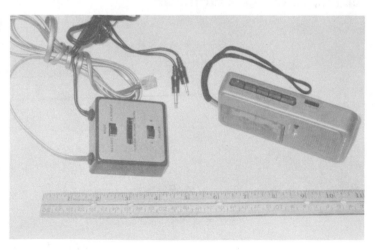

Goof-proof, cheap, and very easy to use, this system is commonly used by spouses and some professionals to tap phones.

There are some other methods that might be used against you if the phone tapper is technically inclined. Any second- or third-rate electronics hobbyist can build a radio frequency telephone tap for less than $10. In most cases, these taps can be placed anywhere along the telephone line (usually off the premises). Radio frequency taps have a typical range of one to two blocks and broadcast both sides of the phone conversation to any "tabletop" FM radio. The FM radio is then connected to a signal-activated switch and then to a tape recorder. For $10 or less, they can also build a high-impedance automatic tape starter and connect it off the premises, somewhere downwire. When it is properly constructed and terminated, not even the Central Intelligence Agency (CIA) will be able to detect it on the line.

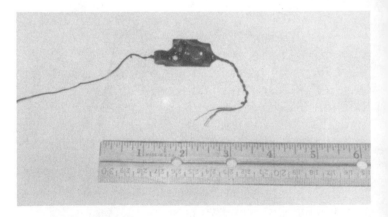

Series radio frequency tap. It draws all of its power from the phone company and transmits both sides of the conversation up to a block from where the phone is in use.

CHAPTER 1
Telephones

Speaking of not being able to detect certain types of high-impedance, parallel taps on a telephone line, back in the 1970s and 1980s, the federal government started spending incredible amounts of money on Data Encryption Standard (DES) encrypted telephones. Bell Labs and Motorola were the prime contractors and were reported to have charged more than $20,000 for each DES-encrypted telephone for the initial production run. Why? The federal government realized that it could not guarantee the integrity of its own phone lines. When in doubt, encrypt!

Here is a method that can be employed by "rogue" law enforcement types or folks with many resources. The operatives may rent or buy a "listening post" somewhere downwire between you and the central switching office. This may be a house, office, garage, or apartment somewhere down the street. If the utilities are aboveground, the operatives will open up a pole-mounted metal box containing connector blocks and jumper your terminal pair with their terminal pair. In the case of underground utilities, the metal box will be mounted on a concrete pad at a street corner, usually within a half mile of your premises. The act of jumpering your wire pair with a listening post wire pair is called a "bridge job." The operatives can then kick back in a comfy, cozy setting and listen and record the intimate details of your life with relative ease.

Another method that can be used by people with means that is less incriminating is to place a radio frequency (RF) tap on your phone line.

Once the RF tap is in place, they can place an FM radio in a car, complete with signal-activated switch and tape recorder, and park the car within two blocks of the RF tap. The operatives will not have to worry if the RF tap is discovered since it is nothing more than a miniature FM broadcast transmitter, and there is no direct connection to the listening post. Another advantage to this type of tapping operation is that the operatives can move the listening post (a van or car) as needed.

Here is another possible method that, I admit, may be a little bit of a stretch. It is entirely possible that the operatives bribed or "got the goods on" a supervisor from the central switching office that services your premises, giving them the ability to tap your line from the

The inside of a subscriber interface or surge protector box.
There's plenty of room for small radio frequency taps to hide.

CO. As stated before, if you're being tapped at the CO, you will not hear the tap, and not even the CIA could detect it on the line.

Telephone tapping is illegal—period. Certain states will not let you record a conversation that you are a party to. My state, Colorado, is a consensual state, which means that I can record anything that I am a party to, as long as I am an active participant in the conversation.

OFFICE TELEPHONES

Tapping of office telephones off premises is not much different from tapping residential telephones off premises. However, there are some differences when it comes to inside wiring and installation of office phone systems. Office phone systems are usually driven by a device know as a "key system unit" that mounts on the wall of a phone closet. In larger systems, it will be a free-standing unit mounted on the floor and referred to as a "switch." Generally, there is one phone closet per floor, and they are usually stacked on top of each other so that wiring can be routed easily.

In a typical phone closet you will find a rat's nest of wires, white R-66 connector blocks, and various key system units, one for each company that occupies a particular floor. As to the purpose of the key system unit: it is an electronic microprocessor-based controller that gives an office all the modern features that most offices cannot live without. It allows you to transfer calls, put people on hold, barge in, conference, use the speaker phone, have music for people on hold, and so on. Now there are also "smart phones" that have all these features built in, but they are usually limited to two or three lines.

Phone closets make excellent tapping points. An operative can get into most phone closets (as of this writing) with a screwdriver. He could just say that he is with a private telecommunications company and make up a ruse that he is doing phone repairs or installation for a company that is a tenant in the building. Most property managers will probably not question him. Of course, using some social engineering and having an honest face will help.

Here is a clever technique that enterprising operatives can employ in a large office building. Suppose the target company has offices on the

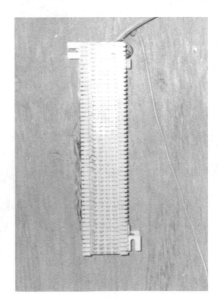

A typical R-66 connector block with 25-pair cable in a phone closet.

eighth floor and the operatives find a vacant suite on the third floor at a low price. The operatives gain access to the phone closets from the third floor to the eighth floor and feed a 25-pair cable from the eighth-floor phone closet to the third-floor phone closet. Some of the wires from the 25-pair cable are discreetly attached to the phone lines of interest in the eighth-floor phone closet. At the third floor, the cable is routed above the ceiling tile from the phone closet over to the third-floor office, where wiretaps are conveniently placed. The operatives can be comfortable and have the dual benefit of being able to do physical surveillance on their target as well as wiretapping him.

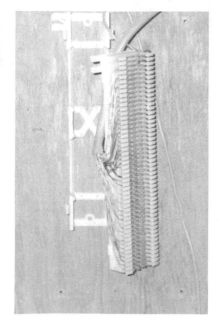

There's plenty of room for an operative to hide a tap behind a typical R-66 connector block.

CHAPTER 2

Cordless

Telephones

The typical cordless phone used in many homes throughout the United States can be intercepted easily by the typical scanner enthusiast. Scanning is a popular hobby in this country. It is estimated that there are 10 million police scanner owners in the United States, which means there is probably a scanner hobbyist on every other block in America. With a typical range of more than a quarter mile, most cordless phone users may be well within range of several scanner owners. Even the cheapest police scanners have the ability to intercept both sides of a cordless phone conversation from more than a block away.

The frequencies of cordless phones were published widely before most of the cordless phones ever hit the marketplace. Scanner hobbyist magazines, electronics magazines, and scanner clubs throughout America sent cordless phone frequency lists to their subscribers. In other words, millions of people with scanners had the frequencies of cordless phones programmed into their scanners back in the early to mid-1980s. For those of you who use or have used cordless phones in the past, please read this paragraph again and weep.

Most cordless phones operate in the frequency range of 46.610 megahertz (MHz) to 46.970 MHz. If an eavesdropper programs his scanner in a search mode from 46.610 to 46.970 MHz, he will be treated to both sides of the conversation. There is a growing number of cordless phones that use the 900 MHz range, as well as those that claim to be "scrambled." But beware, many of the so-called scrambled phones use scrambling techniques that were cracked easily with cheap equipment by electronics hobbyists back in the 1970s. If a scrambled cordless phone uses any kind of "phase inversion" techniques, it's no good. If it uses "digital encryption," it's okay. But keep in mind that wiretappers can always tap the phone line and bypass your scrambled cordless phone.

According to the Electronic Privacy Communications Act (EPCA) of 1986, you have no reasonable expectation of privacy on a cordless phone. Anybody can use cordless phone conversations against you in a court of law. Law enforcement does not need a warrant to listen and record cordless phone conversations. However, if you use a scrambled cordless phone, you have a reasonable expectation of privacy, and law enforcement must obtain a warrant to tap into your line.

In the next section I cover cellular phones. Cellular phones are governed by an entirely different set of laws that hobbyists and law enforcement must abide by. Cellular phones should not be confused with household-type cordless phones. There are significant differences between them.

Update: In October 1995, a law was passed outlawing the monitoring of cordless telephone calls.

CHAPTER 3

Cellular

Telephones

Cellular phones, also called "cell" phones, can be intercepted easily by certain types of police scanners. The typical police scanner nowadays does not have cell phone intercept capabilities, but certain brand-name scanners can be modified easily to receive cell phone conversations. Some very expensive and hard-to-find scanners have cell phone intercept capabilities and do not need modification.

Cell phones operate in the 800 MHz frequency range, but they change frequencies quite often when a person is mobile. When a cell phone changes frequency, it is because the person is moving into another cell location. There are hundreds of frequencies in a typical cell phone system, which is quite a hassle for an eavesdropper who is trying to listen in. In a big city, there may be hundreds of cell phone conversations taking place at once in a metro cell system. An eavesdropper would have to sift through hundreds of conversations on a busy work day in order to find his target once he has changed cell locations. Following the frequency change in small towns or isolated communities is easy, like shooting fish in a barrel. But in big cities it's a big hassle.

Computer-aided scanning to the rescue! If an operative has a good scanner with computer interface capabilities, all is not lost. With the addition of a black box, called a DDI (digital data interpreter), and the correct software, an operative can intercept cell phone conversations and follow the call with ease. The cost: $2,000 to $3,000 total, which would include a computer. Law enforcement systems, which have been in use for years, cost $5,000 to $20,000. Certain cell phone companies have installed auxiliary facilities; that is, extra "shacks" equipped with hook-ups for the exclusive use and convenience of law enforcement.

Cell phone frequencies were published in electronics magazines before the phones even hit the market. Tricks and equipment for monitoring cell phones are usually a regular feature in many scanner publications. In 1993, articles started appearing that showed how a cell phone could be "cloned." Someone could actually make a carbon copy of your cell phone or somebody else's cell phone. If a switch is installed, the eavesdropper could turn off the microphone and listen in. But when the target person was done talking, the eavesdropper could turn the microphone back on and then use the cloned cell phone to make calls to Aunt Tilly in Timbuktu. The bill would then be sent to the target.

According to the Electronic Communications Privacy Act of 1986, it is illegal to listen in on cellular phone conversations. Law enforcement must obtain a warrant in order to monitor cell phone conversations.

CHAPTER 4

Pagers

V oice pagers let you leave a vocal message for the recipient, while digital pagers only show a number on the pager.

Voice pagers have provided hours of listening pleasure and fun over the years for scanning enthusiasts. Many voice pages have been intercepted and mayhem has ensued (use your imagination). Here's an example: "Hey John, this is Joe again. You know, the guy from Tile Works Unlimited? Say, John, I goofed. The work order says that you are to lay the green tiles upstairs and the red ones downstairs." (Trust me, I never played this trick on a floor installation contractor.)

Special interception equipment for digital pagers has been distributed to law enforcement personnel for many years. Its cost has hovered in the $10,000 plus range; however, in 1993 a device was advertised in a nationally distributed communications magazine and is being sold to consumers for $400. This device hooks up to a scanner and an optional printer. The consumer can then receive other people's digital pages. So much for efficient use of tax dollars.

Here is a technique that law enforcement personnel can use to intercept pages. When the cops arrest a suspect, they copy down the CAP code (an internal pager company code for each particular pager) and number from the suspect's pager and then give the pager back to the suspect and let him go. The cops could then go down to the pager carrier, warrant in hand. The pager carrier (usually a regional Bell) will make a clone of the suspect's pager for the cops so they can receive every page that the suspect receives. If the cops have a good rapport with the pager company, the warrant process may be bypassed with a wink and a nod. Certain pager companies are very aggressive in their cooperation with law enforcement.

Pager interception can be of great value in the "spy game." It does not take very long to pinpoint movements, times, dates, activities, phone numbers of other suspects, and more. When you have the phone number, you can get the address, if you know where to look. Digital pagers do not offer much more security than voice pagers.

According to the Electronic Communications Privacy Act of 1986, it is illegal to intercept voice pager or digital pager messages. Law enforcement must obtain a warrant.

CHAPTER 5

Fax

Machines

F ax machine transmissions are easy to intercept if you have the right equipment. The easy way to intercept fax transmissions is to use another fax machine and attach it to the target's phone line. One could also obtain fax interception equipment from law enforcement supply companies for thousands of dollars; however, private operatives and technophiles have been intercepting fax transmissions at a fraction of this cost. If your phone line is being tapped by a law enforcement agency or by some private party with the means and technical ability, chances are that your fax transmissions are being read also.

Fax transmissions have the advantage of eliminating the "casual snoop" and people with little money or technical expertise. However, if the person or agency has the motive, means, and opportunity, intercepting fax transmissions is a cinch.

It is illegal to tap fax transmissions. Law enforcement must obtain a warrant.

CHAPTER 6

Data

Transmissions—

Computer

Modems

All that applies to fax transmissions also applies to data transmissions. A growing number of people are using DES encryption programs in order to send private messages known as e-mail to their friends and associates. Most DES encryption programs are very easy to use and give a very high degree of privacy for data transmissions. One might ask, who could break a DES-encrypted data transmission? The answer: a federal law enforcement agency with a Cray computer. The time frame: two hours to forever, depending on how the transmission was encrypted. There are some very simple techniques for making DES-encrypted transmissions very secure. One is to double encrypt.

The more people who use DES or stronger methods of encryption, the more difficult it will become for authorities or private operatives to eavesdrop on private data transmissions. When it gets to the point where most people are using encrypted transmissions on the information highway, it's going to be almost impossible for Big Brother to keep tabs on us. Talk about information overload and fried Cray computers!

It is illegal to tap data transmissions. Law enforcement officers must obtain a warrant.

CHAPTER 7

Computer

Screens

Some of you are going to have a hard time believing that it is possible to read a computer or TV screen from more than a block away. Decades ago, a man by the name of Van Eck displayed simple homemade equipment that could read a computer screen from a distance. This demonstration was held in a public forum and was not well publicized. "Van Eck" is the term now used widely to describe the technique for reading computer screens from a distance.

A company once offered to sell me a complete Van Eck system for $3,000. For an industrial spy or a government agency, three grand is a drop in the bucket.

Even if you use good communications security, like digital encryption, it is possible for somebody with a Van Eck system to read your message from more than a block away before the message is encrypted. If you are a major drug dealer, mobster, or an outspoken radical who believes very strongly in the U.S. Constitution and you are using DES encryption on a regular basis, government agents will probably use a Van Eck system against you.

The only known way to prevent Van Eck eavesdropping is to use Tempest Standards. (Van Eck is also called "Tempest Attack.") Tempest Standards are a complicated form of shielding and grounding to prevent stray electromagnetic fields from emanating beyond computer and other communications devices. You must know what you are doing if you are going to employ Tempest precautions. You could build an expensive Tempest room, only to find out too late that you forgot to unplug the phone line from the modem before you encrypted a critical message. Believe it or not, a phone line, an electrical line, or a water pipe leading into the Tempest room can act as an antenna.

You're probably wondering if I have actually seen a real Tempest Attack. Quite frankly, no. However, I have run some crude tests and interviewed many individuals over the years whom I trust, and I am convinced beyond a shadow of a doubt that it is possible to read a computer screen from up to a block away. For those of you who are still skeptical, consider this question: why has the government created a Tempest Standard and spent hundreds of millions of dollars on Tempest Attack prevention? I rest my case.

CHAPTER 8

Covert

Video

Surveillance

As of 1994, electronics hobbyist magazines were advertising video cameras that are 1 inch by 1 inch by 1/2 inch and video transmitters the size of a quarter and 3/8 of an inch in thickness. Add a 9-volt battery and you can transmit video up to and possibly exceeding a one-block range. Just imagine the possible hiding places: ball caps, stuffed animals, table lamps, radios, TVs, motor vehicles—the variety is limited only by one's imagination.

Some well established companies install pinhole lens video cameras. These companies have been installing covert video systems in retail stores, offices, industrial facilities, and government buildings for many years. This is a big business, and it's far more widespread than security personnel care to admit. Covert video cameras can be built into sprinkler heads and passive infrared motion detectors. Pinhole lenses can be installed in a ceiling in such a way that you could stare at the ceiling for hours and not be able to see the lens.

What is particularly disturbing about these systems is that they can be installed by virtually anybody, without requiring any technical skill beyond the ability to use a screwdriver. The price is well within the reach of the typical consumer. At this writing, there are no laws against video surveillance in the United States, with the exception that you cannot install it in a bathroom or any kind of changing room.

The U.S. government has had the ability to read a newspaper headline from a satellite for many years now. From a satellite "heat signatures" can be read anywhere under its "footprint." In layman's terms, if you're on a mission in a wilderness area, or even an abandoned urban area, and you start a small campfire or light a small camping stove, even inside a small, uninsulated building, it will show up. Furthermore, these satellites make regular heat signature comparisons, and they will alert their operators.

Satellite technology has progressed to the point that it can detect a definite heat signature difference between cut vegetation and live vegetation. If you are sleeping in a tent, your general outline can be seen from a satellite. Some possible ways to avoid these satellite intrusions are to conduct your operations on a very cloudy day or night, sleep in a cave, or stay in a heavy forest with a thick canopy of live vegetation above you. You could also heap a layer of dirt on a small abandoned building and use it as a temporary refuge. A cheap aluminized mylar survival blanket, sold at sporting goods stores, can do wonders when used properly.

Video cameras that were marketed in the 1980s were rather bulky, and they did not work very well in low light conditions. By the late

Video transmitter with 100-yard range. This can be used with a small CCD video camera and a 9-volt battery pack. There are units available (with miniature video camera included) that are a quarter of the size shown here.

1980s, surveillance buffs started to discover that the new charged coupled device (CCD) video cameras could operate well under low light conditions. CCD video cameras have another advantage over the standard tube type consumer-grade video cameras—they can be made much smaller. Because of CCD technology, the small size that I described earlier was achieved.

Spotlight with infrared lens. With the lens on, you cannot see any light with the naked eye. When you use it with a night vision scope, you can illuminate a suspect in a dark corner of a yard or an alley without his being aware that he is being observed.

CCD video cameras can see infrared light sources. An infrared TV remote looks like a little penlight through a CCD video camera. A surveillance operative who needs to get choice video under very low light conditions will use a CCD video camera and an infrared light source. The light source could be as simple as a spotlight with an infrared filter covering the spotlight lens. An unsuspecting person can be fully illuminated and not have a clue that every move he makes is being observed with ease using CCD video or night vision devices. (You cannot see infrared light with the naked eye.)

There are two very general terms for describing night vision devices.

1) Active—This type requires an infrared light source in order to be of any use. This was the first night vision device.

2) Passive—This type is commonly referred to as "starlight," because it only requires starlight or moonlight to operate. It will actually amplify starlight and moonlight by a very large magnification factor. It's been around for decades and is the most popular of the two. Starlight scopes have adapters that permit their use with tube-type video cameras. Starlight scopes can be enhanced for very low light situations by adding an infrared light source.

Let's do a little "reverse engineering." If you obtain a starlight scope (for $500 from Russian surplus), you can scan your rooms, yard, and neighborhood for any infrared light sources. Perhaps you can also get a glimpse of someone sneaking around your neighborhood with your night vision scope. It's fun and educational to scan one's "turf."

Surplus starlight night vision scope. It's great for spotting infrared light sources. You can see an infrared bug or an infrared remote control from more than a block away at night.

CHAPTER 9

Bugging

There are hundreds, perhaps thousands, of ways to bug conversations.

AMATEUR BUGGING

The following are samples of the ways in which an individual with limited funds and limited technical skill could bug a room.

The amateur bugger could purchase a wireless baby monitor and hide it in his home, office, apartment, or other room of interest behind a large, rarely moved appliance or piece of behind a large, rarely moved appliance or piece of furniture. He can be up to a block away and listen in on all the conversations in the room of interest with the companion receiver, which is normally sold with the baby monitor. Baby monitors are quite sensitive, and they are usually crystal controlled, which prevents frequency drift. However, they tend to be a little bit bulky.

The supervisor of an office or warehouse could buy an intercom system, either wired or wireless, and put the master unit in his office and the slave unit in an employee's work area. The supervisor could cleverly conceal the slave unit in the employee area if he is worried about its being discovered. He could then sit back and listen in on the employee's conversations. How many of us have fallen victim to this trick over the years?

Wireless studio or lapel microphones are readily available at certain electronic outlets and audio-visual rental shops. The cheap units have up to a 300-foot range, and the expensive units have up to a 1/4-mile range under the right conditions. Some of the very expensive units are drift free, use two antennas, and are called "diversity microphone systems."

Wireless microphones are like miniature broadcast stations. Legally, they should be worn on your body—that's why they are also referred to as "body mics." I have seen some cheaper units demonstrated and can attest to the fact that if you set them down in a room, they will pick up a whisper from 15 feet or more and broadcast it up to 200 feet away. Most of these studio or body mics come with a companion receiver. Some nasty people have been known to hide these mics in rooms.

• • •

The three devices listed above are very inexpensive. Wireless baby monitors are available for $60 or less, wireless intercoms for $80 or less, hard-wired intercoms for as little as $15, and cheap body mic systems for as little as $49 (including body mic and receiver). These products are usually available seven days a week all over the United States. Wireless baby monitor reception can be greatly improved by using a police scanner with an outside antenna instead of the supplied receiver.

Professionals who use crystal-controlled (drift-free) transmitters will typically use a scanner.

Operations

Here are some examples of how an amateur might operate. He could buy a bug through underground sources or purchase a bug kit with some assembly required from various suppliers that advertise in electronics magazines. Believe it or not, it is illegal to possess or transport a device that can be "primarily useful" for eavesdropping purposes; however, it is legal to sell or buy a bug or tap in kit form. Baby monitors, intercoms, and body transmitters are exempt from the law, as long as they are used in the manner for which they were intended.

If a person is able to use a soldering iron and is mechanically inclined, he will not have to know electronics in order to assemble some of

This small bugging transmitter can be thrown together with $4 worth of parts. It uses a small button cell battery and can pick up a whisper from 20 feet and broadcast it up to 1/2-mile away.

these kits; however, frequency adjustment for their ideal operation can be quite difficult. He could hire an electronics technician to assemble the bug kit and do the necessary adjustments in order to avoid any technical difficulties.

Many commercial bugs and kit form bugs are very small, usually 3/4 inch x 1/2 inch. Most of the time, the 9-volt battery that the bug is attached to is actually much bigger than the bug. An operative has a distinct disadvantage when using battery-operated bugs because they tend to use up the battery in three days or less, depending on the efficiency and overall design of the bug. Small bugs that use AC (alternating current) power are rare and are quite a bit more difficult for the amateur to place.

The transmission range of most bugs is 200

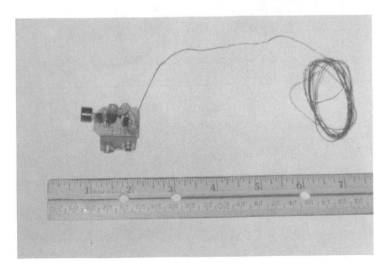

A typical 9-volt bugging transmitter.

feet to 1 mile, depending on the transmitter's design, terrain, antenna, and the receiving setup. Do not believe advertised transmission ranges. Incorrectly adjusted bugs may only transmit up to 50 feet, or not at all.

Techniques

An operative could place a bug anywhere in a room in a hidden location, preferably away from large metal objects. Close proximity to

Amateurs and some professionals will typically use a standard tabletop portable radio with or without an automatic frequency conrol (AFC). Radios with standard analog tuning are required when the transmitter is not crystal controlled.

metal objects can be very disruptive to small bugging transmitters. The operative could connect two or more batteries in parallel for greater transmission time, that is, four days instead of two. The hiding places for bugs this small are too numerous to list. They are limited only by one's imagination and mechanical/ electrical ability. Once the bugging transmitter is placed, all the operative has to do is set up a listening post. The listing post could be a vehicle, rented office, garage, house, or apartment. A tabletop portable FM radio, a signal-activated switch, and a tape recorder is all that is needed for automatic operation.

A variation of the above technique is a properly placed VOX (voice-operated) transmitter and a radio with a VOX tape recorder. The beauty of this system is that the bug does not transmit unless someone is talking or making noise. Detection of a VOX-operated bug is somewhat reduced since it is on only when someone is talking. When someone walks into the room and starts talking, the VOX-operated transmitter starts transmitting to the FM radio at the listening post and then the VOX-operated tape recorder starts to record. It is totally automatic and relatively simple to do.

Can you think of any ways that these automatic recording systems can be sabotaged? (Think before you peek ahead to the next sentence.) You could turn on a radio, TV, or stereo and just leave it on all day and night. The poor bugger will have tape after tape of nothing but garbage. Chances are, any sensitive room conversations will be garbled if a TV or stereo in the target room is turned up loud enough. It is very difficult to listen in on conversations in the presence of loud background noise. Even the pros have a difficult time filtering out loud background noise and separating it from the conversation.

Another time-honored method of bugging by

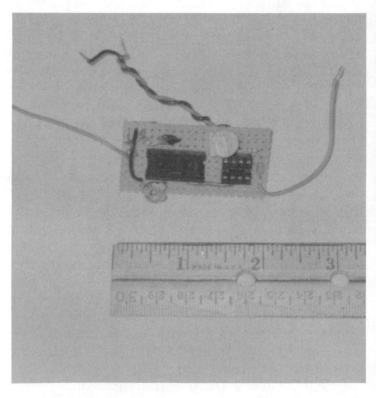

Subcarrier converter. This unit (integrated circuits removed) can easily convert any 6- to 18-volt bugging transmitter to subcarrier operation.

Tabletop portable radio with homemade subcarrier decoder on top.

an amateur is to use carrier current transmitters that use very low frequencies (below the AM broadcast band). These transmitters use a building's wiring for their power and signal path. They rarely transmit much beyond the building that they are installed in. The operative could rent an office or apartment in the target's building and then hide a carrier current transmitter in the target's room. The beauty of this system is that the transmitter will last indefinitely, and most so-called countermeasures personnel probably will not detect it.

Most over-the-counter counter-measures gear is not designed to detect these low frequencies.

Most generic hidden transmitter locators sold in the United States will not work very well in urban and suburban areas due to the high levels of radio frequency energy floating around. A good countermeasures team will always use a spectrum analyzer, which looks similar to an oscilloscope.

Another technique that might be used by an amateur is a very unique bugging device that has been around since the early 1960s. It has many names, but here are just a few: "infinity transmitter," "harmonica bug," and "coast-to-coast transmitter." Back in the 1960s and 1970s, before the phone company switched over to its new electronic switching service (ESS) system, an infinity transmitter could be connected to a phone line and hidden in a room on the target's premises. The operative could call it from anywhere in the world, send a certain tone with a portable tone generator over the phone line, and the device would answer and treat the operative to all the conversations in the room—all without disturbing the normal operation of the phone or alerting the target. The infinity transmitter would answer before the first ring. When the target picked up the phone, everything would go back to normal again.

Once the phone company upgraded the phone system from the old crossbar system to the new ESS system, the older infinity transmitters became useless and could only be used on a second dedicated line. Certain companies have redesigned infinity transmitters so that they will work on the new ESS phone systems; however, they have certain telltale signs: one ring and then less than two minutes later, another ring. If the target picks up the phone after the first ring, it will disrupt the operation of the device, causing the operative to initiate another activation cycle. In other words, he will have to start all over again.

If an operative uses an old-style infinity transmitter with the new phone lines, the phone will ring once and then anybody who tries to call while the infinity transmitter is activated will just get a busy signal. Another problem that can occur when somebody tries to call is that the phone will ring only once and the infinity transmitter will answer. The poor caller will be treated to five to ten seconds of room sounds or conversation before the "timeout" (hang-up sequence). The new generation of "smart" infinity transmitters will disconnect when someone calls, thereby allowing the phone to ring.

The old-style infinity transmitters still have their uses, though. Many homes, apartments, and offices have extra phone lines wired throughout them. All an operative would need to do is hook up an infinity transmitter and conceal it in the target room. After it is hooked up to a spare phone line wire pair, the phone company can be called and told to activate the spare line and assign it an unlisted phone number. The phone bill for this extra line could be sent to a dummy address or even to the target. I doubt if most people would ever notice if they were being billed for an extra phone line.

PROFESSIONAL BUGGING

Now let's look at how a pro might bug someone. Most of the hidden transmitter methods that were mentioned previously will probably take on a new dimension.

Operations

The pro may build or obtain a circuit that will make any battery-operated transmitter AC operated. In other words, it will operate off of 110-volt AC house current and last indefinitely. The pro might build or buy circuits that will allow him to shut off the bug remotely if he hears a person conducting a countermeasures sweep. He may hide many bugs, some very obvious that are meant to be found and others very well hidden and shut off remotely. If a transmitter is shut off remotely, there is nothing to detect.

The pro may use exotic modulation methods for his transmitters that might not be demodulated or detected by most counter-measures teams. A countermeasures team may think that what it is detecting is just junk or some kind of interference.

A pro might also use a very low-power transmitter that may slip past detection. Because there are so many radio and TV signals floating around most metro areas, a low-power transmitter signal might get lost in the shuffle, so to speak. The pro could use a simple relay setup: a low-power bug, a nearby receiver (75 to 200 feet away), and a more powerful relay transmitter connected to the receiver, which then retransmits to another receiver located much farther away (two blocks to two miles).

Techniques

A pro might use "hard-wired" techniques, which simply means that the microphone is wired directly to the listening post where the tape recorder is sitting. There are microphones that you would need tweezers to handle, and they can be connected with either very fine wire or conductive paint. A real clever pro might install a tiny microphone, run a long length of

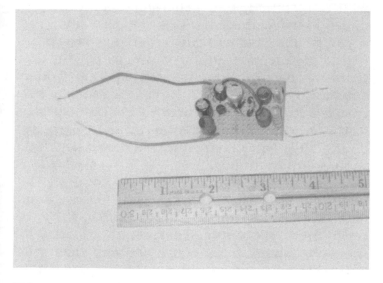

This power converter converts most 6- to 12-volt transmitters to AC operation. Most over-the-counter adapters do not work—this does. (Sorry, not for sale.)

fine wire to it, and then hook up the wires (at the other end) to a hidden transmitter. When the countermeasures team conducts a sweep, it will probably not detect anything because the transmitter is some distance away.

Contrary to what you may have been told by Hollywood or security professionals, microphones cannot be detected without a good physical search. They do not radiate any detectable fields. I have experimented with high-powered ultrasonic fields and high-frequency response tweeters, and I was never able to make a microphone squeal—not ever. If you know somebody who thinks that you can find hidden microphones consistently by bombarding them with ultrasonic sound generators, send them to me and I will sell them a bridge in Brooklyn.

A pro may use a transmitter that is way up in the gigahertz frequency range, beyond the detection capabilities of the typical electronics countermeasures jockey. He may also use a bug that is very low in frequency—200 kilohertz or less. Many electronics countermeasures experts do not have equipment that will detect anything that low in frequency.

Government agents may use some of the techniques as the pros but with these added dimensions: slightly smaller units that are 10 times more expensive. The results are usually the same: intercepted conversations, electronic countermeasures teams with egg on their faces, and very angry clients, some of who end up in the Gray Bar Hotel wearing stripes or orange jumpsuits.

A technique that federal agents have used for years is to hide a pulse burst transmitter in a target's room or office. The pulse burst transmitter stores up conversations and then sends anywhere from seconds to minutes worth of conversation out in one data burst, lasting for a brief instant. The "off air" duration is much longer than the "on air" duration. In other words, it does not transmit very often, which makes it hard to detect. I would like to see the local "rain dancer" who does not know a transistor from a resistor try to find a pulse burst transmitter using a generic hidden transmitter locator.

Another technique used by feds and international spy rings that has been around for decades is passive bugging. It consists of a microwave transmitter and a resonant cavity. The resonant cavity is nothing more than a microwave frequency resonant stripline and a microphone. It has no semiconductors or components at all. It is basically a small circuit board and a microphone. Passive bugs can be built into art objects, walls, or ceilings. They do not need a power source. An operative could be a block or more away and direct a microwave beam at the passive bug and then listen in on any room conversations. Most countermeasures teams will not detect a passive bug job. The Russians pioneered this technique in the 1950s.

Laser bugging is very similar to passive bugging. A laser beam is directed at a window, essentially turning the window into a transducer (microphone). The reflected signal is received at the listening post with a telescope and a very simple light wave receiver. Electronics hobbyists have been experimenting with laser bugging systems for years. They are cheap and relatively easy to assemble. However, the audio quality is fair at best, depending on the window's construction and nearby road noise.

Here is an interesting method that a pro or government agency may use. Some small infrared bugging devices measure 1 inch by 1 inch by 1/2 inch and can pick up a whisper from 20 feet away and then transmit that whisper on an infrared light beam to a listening post one or two blocks away. As stated before, you cannot see an infrared beam with the naked eye. There is one very big problem with this type of bugging system: it requires absolutely accurate line of sight alignment. However, there is one very big advantage to this bugging system: it won't be found by most electronic countermeasures teams.

A transmitter and receiver for an infrared bugging system can be built for less than $25 by a good electronics hobbyist. It may not be as small or as pretty, but it will do the job. I have seen homemade units that are as small as a pack of cigarettes. An operative could hide the unit in another room or even outside the building and then run a very thin cable to a tiny microphone hidden in the target room.

A simple countermeasures trick to detect laser bugging devices is to use a surplus ($500 or less) night vision scope in order to spot the listening post. If you are brave enough to visit

Cigarette pack-sized infrared bugging transmitter. It has a provision for a remote microphone. It is hard to aim and even harder to hide, but it will be missed by most counter-measures technicians.

the listening post, bring a rather large friend with you. The pros use lasers with beams that are not visible to the naked eye. Never look directly into a laser beam.

To find out if there is an infrared bugging device in or around your home or office, just take a night vision scope and scan the outside of the building. The infrared bug will look like a little pocket flashlight beam emanating from the building.

Here is another method of bugging used by law enforcement and pros. There is a device that has been available for many years from law enforcement suppliers and underground sources. It's commonly referred to as a combination room monitoring and telephone tap transmitter. This device is small enough to be installed inside a typical telephone. When the phone is hung up, the device will transmit any room conversations, and when the phone is being used, it will transmit any phone conversations. You might call it a "double your pleasure, double your fun bug." The typical advertised range on this type of transmitter is two blocks or more.

Let's not forget vehicle bugging. There are some very effective bugs made just for bugging vehicles, which are usually placed in line with the vehicle's radio antenna. These units are typically sold to law enforcement complete with an automated receiving system.

CHAPTER 10

Bumper

Beepers

A bumber beeper is a small tracking device that is placed in or around a vehicle and transmits an intermittent beep via radio frequency. This radio signal is then received with radio direction finding equipment.

The typical bumper beepers sold to security personnel and private investigators usually have disappointing transmission ranges. Never believe the advertised ranges of transmitters. I personally tested two systems in the past, and I was very disappointed. The typical range in a suburban neighborhood was one to two blocks.

In an urban (big city) environment, the range was less than one block. Almost all of the private investigators I have interviewed since the early 1980s have also stated that they were very disappointed with the bumper beeper systems they had used.

Law enforcement tracking systems are quite an improvement over the typical systems sold to private investigators. The Federal Communications Commission gives much more leeway to law enforcement when it comes to power output (higher power equals longer range) and frequency of operation. Systems made exclusively for law enforcement have ranges in excess of 5 miles for land vehicles and 20 miles or more for aircraft.

Some law enforcement tracking devices have rather unique features and can be activated remotely. Some units transmit a short series of beeps and then shut down for 5 to 15 minutes. If the unit shuts down for this long, a countermeasures team will probably not detect the tracking device. Most people assume that tracking devices transmit a steady series of beeps and do not expect them to have a long shutdown period. Sometimes these units are hidden in contraband cargo.

For those of you who own a police scanner, here are some general frequency ranges for you to scan.

30 MHz to 46 MHz (local and state police)

153.74 MHz to 156.24 MHz (local and state police)

158.730 MHz to 159.465 MHz (local and state police)

162 MHz to 174 MHz (federal government)

406 MHz to 420 MHz (federal government)

453 MHz to 454 MHz (local police and government)

460 MHz to 460.625 MHz (local police)

Try using a search mode and lots of patience. In the frequency ranges listed, you will hear a variety of communications: undercover, local and state government, and possibly bumper beepers. In the federal government frequency ranges you may hear transmissions that sound like a rush of white noise followed by a high-pitched "ping." The white noise is DES encryption—more than likely the agency is using Motorola brand two-way radio units for voice communications.

By law, you must keep communications interceptions to yourself, unless it's a Mayday (distress) call.

CHAPTER 11

Miscellaneous

Some large modern office phone systems have some severe vulnerabilities that operatives who are familiar with these systems can exploit. Some systems have a feature known as "executive override." When this feature is programmed in by the telecommunications technician, the top executive can call any extension in the building, punch in a special code, and then listen in on any employee's phone conversation. The executive does not have to be in the building—he could be calling from anywhere. The technician can also disable the "executive override alerting tone" so that the victim would not be aware that somebody was listening in.

These systems can be turned into infinity transmitters with proper programming and some physical modifications. Simply stated, someone could call in from the outside (anywhere) and access the "hands free" feature of the speaker phone. Just imagine, someone on a beach in Maui being able to call your extension and listen in on your office conversations. These techniques have been known to professionals for many years now. Some of these systems have major brand names, which I will not mention here. Hackers love a challenge, and I am quite certain that many technophiles are aware of these modern office phone system vulnerabilities. It's just another playground for them.

There is a simple bugging technique that turns the typical residential telephone into a standing microphone. The operative can modify a residential telephone in several minutes or less and can sit safely downwire with a portable amplifier or tape recorder and listen to your room conversations. Most people would never notice this modification. There are also spike microphones and uniquely designed transducers that can turn a wall or heating and cooling duct work into a microphone.

Since the 1960s, the phone company has had a system known as Automatic Message Accounting (AMA). This system keeps a record of all calls made, local as well as long distance, and makes a time, date, and number dialed record, even on local calls. The phone company was very tight-lipped about AMA for many years, even with the authorities.

Any trash left at the curbside is "fair game," according to the supreme court. Professional garbologists have told me that they can gain a wealth of information from someone's trash. It would be a good practice to destroy utility bills, memos, and any personal correspondence instead of throwing them out.

CHAPTER 12

A Message Encryption System for Everyone

Here is a very cheap and effective way to send messages, either verbal or written.

1) Buy two, very old, identical obscure books or magazines.

2) Hide one of them in an old notebook, newspaper, or brown paper sack, and hand it to one of your trusted associates.

3) The code goes like this:

P# means page number
S# means line or sentence number (I prefer line number)
L# means letter number

The quick brown fox jumped over the moon to fetch a pail of water. The quick brown fox vaporized due to the fact that outer space is a perfect vacuum. His proverbial "goose" was cooked, so to speak, even though outer space is freezing cold.

Coded message:

P1 S1 L19	L3	L3	L1	L41	L1	L7	L11	L5	L10	L1	L2	L11	L5	S2 L47	S1 L3
m	e	e	t	a	t	c	o	u	r	t	h	o	u	s	e

Page #1

Sentence #1

Sentence #2

Sentence #1

The story of the spaced-out fox.

Cumbersome? Yes. Secure and cheap? A definite yes. For security reasons, do not designate any space or demarcation between words. Your associate at the receiving end should have the smarts to separate the words. The old, identical books or magazines (known as the "keys") should be changed every now and then. This code is nearly unbreakable as long as the enemy does not know what books or magazines you and your associates are using.

CHAPTER 13

Dirty Tricks

to Play on

Buggers and

Tappers

The following is a list of simple dirty tricks to play on eavesdroppers.

1) Turn radios, TVs, and stereos on. Most bugging devices will be overwhelmed and the audio quality turned to mud with loud-playing home entertainment devices. Stand or sit close to the person you are conversing with, and keep your voices down. Make sure that

the person is not wired.

2) Use writing pads. If the people doing the bugging have good audio filtering (processing) equipment, use writing pads and burn or flush the top sheet and the sheet underneath the top sheet.

3) If you leave a home or office that may be bugged, leave the radio or TV on. Any voice-activated bugging devices will turn on and record many hours of garbage.

4) Use different phone booths. You and your associates should have some prearranged phone booth locations. Do not discuss phone and meeting locations on a phone that you think may be tapped.

5) Take the phone off the hook on a random basis, and place the handset close to a stereo speaker playing some totally obnoxious music. Just think of the many hours of listening pleasure that some poor wiretapper is going to be subjected to.

6) Avoid using cordless phones, and insist that your contacts avoid using them.

7) Use a voice disguising telephone. It will make your voice totally unrecognizable. This defeats voice analysis and is less incriminating. The price of voice disguising equipment has really dropped (it's less than $100 now).

8) If you are having a meeting and discussing sensitive subjects in either an office or a residence, unplug the telephone from the wall jack. This will defeat any telephone instrument modifications.

Warning: Most generic hidden transmitter locators and wiretap detectors do not work very well in most situations. Other than a very expensive TDR (time domain reflectometer, a sophisticated cable fault locator costing $5,000 and up), all of the generic telephone line tap detectors that I have ever tested are worthless when detecting phone line taps off premises.

CHAPTER 14

Common

Misconceptions

MISCONCEPTION **#1**: "I have been told that a good countermeasures team can tell if my telephone is tapped at the phone company's central switching office."

FACT: False. Electronically, there is no way to tell if there is a tap at the CO. The electrical characteristics of the phone line may vary from one central switching office to another. I have personally seen situations where 300 feet off the premises a phone line was interfaced with a T-1 carrier system, which will read like a parallel connected wiretap. A T-1 carrier system is a sophisticated method for putting multiple conversations and fax/data transmissions on one phone line pair and is used by the phone company to save on new telephone line installation expenses. It is generally used when the cost of running new lines is very inconvenient or cost prohibitive. Central switching office equipment will look like a telephone tap on a TDR.

MISCONCEPTION #2: "Some people have said that they can hear most telephone taps."

FACT: This wild (but common) misconception almost warrants not being dignified with an answer. Unless some wiretapper is a complete moron and is using defective equipment connected in an improper manner, there will be no audible noise generated by the tap. Most of us can hear an extension phone when it is lifted from the cradle—a drop in the audio level occurs because of a drop in voltage across the phone line. However, most telephone taps, no matter how simple their construction, will be totally inaudible to the victim.

MISCONCEPTION #3: "I have been told that there is a number that I can dial that will tell me immediately and with certainty if my phone is tapped."

FACT: The only deserving answer for a person who believes this one is, "I have some oceanfront property for sale in Arizona."

MISCONCEPTION #4: "Any countermeasures team chosen at random from the phone book will be able to find a telephone tap on my phone line, assuming it has been tapped."

FACT: False. There are at least three methods of telephone tapping that will not be detected by the best, most sophisticated intelligence agencies in the world. One method costs $50, one cost $5 or less, and one costs 50¢ or less. The only way to find these devices is to inspect every linear foot of cable from the phone to the central switching office. Not only is this physically impossible, you would be trespassing on phone company property. In the case of underground utilities, not even the CIA would be able to get permission to dig up miles of phone cable. Most counter-measures teams do not know a transistor from a resistor and do not have a clue as to the basic phone line electrical parameters.

MISCONCEPTION #5: "Any countermeasures team should be able to tell if my telephone has been bugged."

FACT: False. Certain telephones on the market, which may be identical to the one you are currently using, have been altered in such a way that not even the company who manufactured the phone could tell if it was modified for bugging purposes. It has been reported that the small network boxes in the older style (2500 series) phones could be replaced with modified network boxes that will place room conversations on the line when activated remotely. A physical search will do no good in these situations.

MISCONCEPTION #6: "It is my under-standing that a countermeasures team should be able to debug my home or office in two hours or less."

FACT: False. A half a day to one full day is typical. Anything less than four hours would make me suspicious of the countermeasures team.

CHAPTER 15

Choosing a Countermeasures Person

Here is a short list of questions that you should ask a prospective counter-measures person.

1) Does he know the basics of the frequency spectrum, basic frequency allocations, and basic propagation characteristics of commonly used frequencies?

2) Does he own a police scanner and use it on a regular basis? Is short-wave listening and scanning

an ongoing hobby of his? If not, was it ever his hobby at any time?

3) Does he know the approximate band width of his radio detection equipment (hidden transmitter locators)?

4) What kind of equipment does he use to find hidden trans-mitters? Does he use a spectrum analyzer?

5) If he does not use a spectrum analyzer, does he at the very least use a near field receiver along with various radios that cover a wide portion of the frequency spectrum?

6) Will he let you watch? If not, definitely call someone else!

7) Did he tell you that there are certain bugs that cannot be found unless you literally tear the place apart?

8) Has he done any electronic experimentation and design work?

If he answers "no" to any of questions 1, 2, 3, 5, or 6, search for another debugger.

If your main concern is with phone tapping, here are some questions you should ask.

1) Has he ever done any office or residential phone installation?

2) Does he understand the basic electrical characteristics of

phone lines: voltage, current, impedance, and so on?

3) Is he aware of the fact that certain taps cannot be detected?

If his answer is "no" to any of these questions, look for someone else. Beware, he might lie about his experience. *Do not talk on a phone that might be compromised!*

CHAPTER 16

Legal

Considerations

I learned early on in the countermeasures business that your chances of winning the lottery are greater than finding a lawyer who is knowledgeable about communications privacy laws. I have met many private investigators, lawyers, and security personnel who are not even aware of the fact that bugging and tapping are illegal. Most people do not realize that you must be a party (participant) to a conversation in order to record it, according to federal law. Certain states do not allow you to record conversations even if you are a participant. It would be a good idea to check state as well as federal laws.

Back in 1968, Congress enacted the Omnibus Crime Control and Safe Streets Act. This law made bugging and telephone tapping illegal. Before this law was passed, it was a "free for all" for inquisitive minds. I remember there being catalogs filled with ads for bugging transmitters and a wide variety of telephone tapping devices for sale prior to 1968. According to the law (not actual practice), the only people who can bug and tap anybody are those in the government, provided that they have a proper warrant signed by a judge.

In 1986, Congress brought us a "new, improved" communications privacy law, updated for the new communications technologies. This law is called the Electronic Communications Privacy Act of 1986. For the first time in the history of the United States, certain frequencies were made illegal to monitor. Cellular phone monitoring and certain pager modes were declared off limits to people with scanners. Many valiant constitutionalists argued intelligently against this draconian provision, but in the end, the cellular lobbyists with briefcases full of political action committee (PAC) money won the battle against them.

The constitutionalists argued that if you want privacy, you should encrypt your communications. Since these communications are broadcast over the public airwaves and permeate our homes, offices, and bodies, we have a right to monitor these frequencies. Old TVs and VCRs do a fair job of picking up nearby cell phone conversations, so how do you police this absurd provision in the law? The bottom line is, cell phone companies can now sell their clients a false sense of security at the expense of our constitutional rights.

In the ECPA of 1986, Congress allowed the monitoring of household cordless phones because they use the public airwaves and "you have no reasonable expectation of privacy." (No PAC money here!)

It is estimated that for every legal, court-ordered electronic surveillance conducted by law enforcement, there are at least 100 illegal electronic surveillance operations conducted by lawmen, which are known as "wildcat" operations. Can this be proven? Not in our lifetime. One way that it can be proven theoretically is as follows: The number of court-ordered electronic surveillance operations conducted by law enforcement each year is a matter of public record. If you look at the number of suppliers of spy gear, sold only to law enforcement, and do a rough estimate of their production capabilities, you will find that 100 to 1 is not so farfetched.

It is a matter of public record that 800 to 900 court-ordered electronic surveillance operations are conducted by law enforcement each year. Now here is one of my favorite examples of how we can prove the 100 to 1 (or more) theory: If a one-man shop can produce 5,000 bugs and taps per year with weekends off, then imagine what a company like AID of Florida, which makes surveillance equipment for law enforcement, can produce with its 200 employees and its economies of scale. There are dozens of companies like AID around the globe that sell to law enforcement only.

Most of us streetwise countermeasures folks just about fall out of our chairs when we see these published statistics on the number of court-ordered wiretaps. If you have some long talks with honest ex-lawmen, you will quickly realize that these 800 to 900 reported court-ordered electronic surveillance operations are just the tip of the iceburg. Perhaps 100 illegal operations to 1 legal operation may be under-stating the fact.

YOU AND THE PHONE COMPANY

It is illegal for the phone company to notify you if law enforcement is tapping your phone line legally. The problem with this is that phone company personnel do not know whether it is a legal tap or not. Phone workers do not want to risk jail time, so what do they do? They keep their mouths shut. They tell you that everything is okay. If it looks like a law enforcement tap, they will say that they found nothing.

According to the ECPA of 1986, the phone company, long-distance companies, and private switchboard operators can legally monitor your conversations in order to spot check the quality of the line and to prevent fraudulent use of their facilities. Does anyone see any potential for abuses here? Like ratting you out to the government or getting an insider trading tip from listening to your conversation with a stockbroker?

CHAPTER 17

The Future of Telephone Tapping

At some point in the near future, the phone company is going to replace copper wire phone lines with fiber-optic cable. A handful of areas around the country already have fiber optics in place, but most of us are still serviced by copper wire.

It is going to be very difficult for most wiretappers (at this writing) to tap fiber-optic cable. It will require highly specialized technicians with very expensive equipment. Just because someone is adept at assembling a small fiber-optic network purchased from some electronic hobby magazine does not in any way qualify him to be able to tap a fiber-optic cable.

Can a fiber-optic cable be tapped? Yes, definitely. But consider the following: Let's say that you are authorized to tap into a fiber-optic cable. You will find a large bundle of tiny glass fibers, each carrying a potential of thousands of communications per tiny strand. What strand do you tap? When you find the proper strand, you may find hundreds, if not thousands of communications taking place. You will then need some fancy digital equipment in order to select and demodulate the signal of choice. In addition, there may be a sophisticated alarm system in place that will detect a fault or tap in the fiber-optic cable. It will be a lot easier to tap the line at the victim's premises or at the central switching office that services the victim's premises.

The U.S. Congress signed a bill into law in August of 1994 that forces the phone company as well as pager and long distance carriers to upgrade their facilities in order to make it easier for law enforcement to tap phone conversations and fax and data transmissions. When the upgrades are complete, the government will be able to tap phone and fax machines remotely, without having to go to the phone company central switching office. Phone company personnel will be oblivious as to which of their clients are being tapped.

THE CLIPPER CHIP

As of this writing, the government is trying to push the clipper chip on the American people. The government wants this chip to be installed in phones and fax and data transmission equipment. It will encrypt communications, thereby keeping them private. The fatal flaw in it is that the government will have the back door to your communications, although the government will allegedly use a warrant in order to access it and decrypt your communications.

Contrary to a popular rumor floating around, switching to a conventional (analog) type phone will not offer you any protection when the clipper system is in place. Analog phones are very easy to tap.

CHAPTER 18

Interesting

Frequencies

to Monitor

Please note that frequencies and their uses are subject to change without notice. Do not repeat any communications that you intercepted with your scanner.

WIRELESS BODY
MICROPHONE FREQUENCIES

Law enforcement is authorized to use the following frequencies for wireless body microphones:

169.445 MHz
169.505 MHz
170.245 MHz
170.305 MHz
171.045 MHz
171.105 MHz
171.845 MHz
171.905 MHz

Keep in mind that law enforcement may use other frequencies as well. Their range is one city block or less.

Private operative and federal law enforcement wireless body microphones have been reported on the following frequencies.

72 MHz to   76 MHz
174 MHz to 216 MHz

These are usually "diversity" wireless microphone systems that use two receiving antennas at the listening post. Most scanners do not receive these frequencies; however, if you have a tabletop portable radio that covers television channels 2 through 13, just tune slowly through the blank channels. Many electronics stores have a large inventory of radios that tune in TV sound for channels 2 through 13, and most cities have TV channels that are not in use, for example, channels 3, 5, 8, 10, 11, and 13 in Denver, Colorado. Most modern scanners have very fast search rates. It is illegal to monitor federal body transmitters.

Do not forget to search these federal, state, and local government and business frequencies:

---

30 MHz to 50 MHz
108 MHz to 144 MHz
148 MHz to 174 MHz
215 MHz to 512 MHz
894 MHz to 960 MHz

ELECTRONIC APPLIANCE STORE WIRELESS BODY MICROPHONES

These units operate on 49 MHz to 50 MHz and have limited power and a limited range (a half block or less).

With a good scanner and a tabletop radio that tunes TV channels 2 through 13, you should be able to uncover most body transmitters manufactured and sold throughout the United States. In order to listen to wireless body microphones and hidden transmitters, you will generally need to be within a one block radius. An outside antenna will help.

If the operative is using a hidden tape recorder, scanners, radios, and bug detectors will do you no good.

VEHICLE TRACKING DEVICES (BUMPER BEEPERS)

Some police and federal agencies use bumper beepers in the 30.86 MHz to 31.98 MHz frequency range shown below. As stated before, these units may only transmit a short series of beeps once every 5 to 15 minutes. Some patience is required in order to detect these beepers.

30.86 MHz
30.90 MHz
30.94 MHz
30.98 MHz
31.02 MHz
31.06 MHz
31.10 MHz
31.14 MHz
31.18 MHz
31.22 MHz
31.26 MHz
31.30 MHz
31.34 MHz
31.38 MHz
31.42 MHz
31.46 MHz
31.50 MHz
31.54 MHz
31.58 MHz
31.62 MHz
31.66 MHz
31.70 MHz
31.74 MHz
31.78 MHz
31.82 MHz
31.86 MHz
31.90 MHz
31.94 MHz
31.98 MHz

(Notice that the spacing is 40 KHz or .04 MHz.)

The Federal Bureau of Investigation (FBI) has been reported using frequencies 40.17 MHz and 40.22 MHz.

The Secret Service has been reported using frequencies 406.75 MHz, 407.80 MHz, 408.50 MHz, and 408.975 MHz.

The Bureau of Alcohol, Tobacco, and Firearms (BATF) has been reported using frequencies 165.5125 MHz and 170.4125 MHz.

The U.S. Customs Service has been reported using frequencies 164.4625 MHz, 164.8625 MHz, 165.4875 MHz, 166.6625 MHz, and 166.8625 MHz.

Be sure to search out frequencies adjacent to and in between the frequencies listed.

The famous LoJack anti-car-theft vehicle tracking systems use 173.075 MHz. When the police get a stolen vehicle call, a transmitter activates the LoJack bumper beeper. Each bumper beeper has its own unique activation signal that it receives. When activated, the bumper beeper transmits a tone every second. The police use radio direction finding equipment to locate the stolen vehicle. Obviously, not all vehicles are equipped with LoJack systems. Less than half of the states have LoJack systems in place at this writing.

This is by no means a complete list of bumper beeper frequencies. It is just a list of some of the more active frequencies reported around the country.

CHAPTER 19

Conclusion and Some Final Thoughts

This book is not intended to show all of the electronic bugging, tapping, and counter-measures techniques available—just the basics. If you have read up to this point and thoroughly studied this book, you probably know more than most investigators and security personnel. If an operative is determined and has the resources, nobody, not even the CIA, can protect your phone line or the intimate details of your life from being betrayed.

I did a short stint in the telecommunications industry, and I have interviewed various telecommunications workers over the years. I found out that the phone company installed a lot of redundant wire pairs around many metro areas, known as "leftovers." These leftover wire pairs may appear anywhere. For example, there may be an extra cable wired in parallel to your home or office phone cable, which may appear down the street in a phone closet, basement, attic, or crawl space coiled or punched down on connector blocks. These provide excellent wiretap points—very ominous indeed.

If you're dealing in very sensitive matters, you and your associates should look into DES encrypted communications systems. DES encryption programs are very easy to use. If you're not into computing, then just use writing pads and do not forget to burn or flush the sheets when they are no longer needed. Do not throw memos in the trash.

If you liked this book,
you will also want to read these:

BENCH-TESTED CIRCUITS FOR SURVEILLANCE AND COUNTERSURVEILLANCE TECHNICIANS
by Tom Larsen

u're hungry for updated, practical electronic circuits, this is a beggar's banquet. Not only do these ingenious circuits
ome never published – really work, but they're simple, inexpensive and fun. Includes clear explanations and schemat-
plus real-life applications. 5 1/2 x 8 1/2, softcover, photos, illus., 128 pp

#TESTED

MORE BENCH-TESTED CIRCUITS
Innovative Designs for Surveillance and Countersurveillance Technicians
by Tom Larsen

d an incendiary method of destroying inaccessible taps and bugs? Some simple circuits for detecting phone line cuts
usage? Maybe you need to build an undetectable phone tap – or turn one on or off remotely! You'll get all this and
re in Larsen's latest! 8 1/2 x 11, softcover, illus., 72 pp.

#TESTED.2

THE BASEMENT BUGGER'S BIBLE
The Professional's Guide to Creating, Building, and Planting Custom Bugs and Wiretaps
by Shifty Bugman

his rare inside look at the shadowy world of surveillance, you'll see how a pro works and the tools he uses, complete
n blueprints of bugs built for big-time gigs and details of how the jobs went down. A hands-on tutorial bursting with
crete, verifiable data and detailed schematics. 8 1/2 x 11, softcover, photos, illus., 328 pp.

#BBB

THE HOME WORKSHOP SPY
Spookware for the Serious Hobbyist
by Nick Chiaroscuro

re are all of the circuit-board patterns, parts lists and building tips needed to build a sneaky array of bugs, taps, mics
d other forbidden spy toys. These simple designs are for "wire specialists" or anyone interested in knowing about the
ndestine sciences. *For academic study only.* 8 1/2 x 11, softcover, photos, illus., 104 pp.

#HWS

ELECTRONIC CIRCUITS AND SECRETS OF AN OLD-FASHIONED SPY
by Sheldon Charrett

arn from the last of the old-fashioned spies how to build bugs or take advantage of those in place; assemble a DTMF
coder with LCD readout or decode the phone tones without one; construct a red box for free pay phone calls; make a
ystal-controlled FM phone tap; crack answering machine passwords and more. 8 1/2 x 11, softcover, photos, illus.,
8 pp.

#CIRCUITS